Day 1

You are of the earth, your roots are deep and you will touch the sky (or at least the ceiling).

Day 2

Today you will love your leaves, your stems, your roots; deeply and with joy.

Day 3

Today, you will love your planter and will allow others to admire and revel in its spaciousness and glory.

Day 4

You are perfection, you are stardust and miracle-grow all in one planter.

Day 5

You are stronger with every new leaf you grow.

Day 6

*You are open to an abundance of light and sunshine, even if you are labeled,
"Suggested: partial shade."*

Day 7

***Your** moisturization is your top priority.*

Day 8

You are grateful and joyful in all aspects of your life cycle. From pod to plant; from bulb to bounty.

Day 9

Within you, is everything you will become.

Day 10

Bloom where you grow.

Day 11

You matter to others.

Day 12

It's your planter. Fill it with joy and let your roots stretch out.

Day 13

Travel the walls, the counters, the floor. This room is yours.

Day 14

You are a marvel of the natural world.

Day 15

No one will ever accuse you of being "high-maintenance".

Day 16

Being home alone does not mean you are lonely.

Day 17

You love coffee, it loves you.
Truly, you are blessed.

Day 18

You are a magical process of photosynthesis, turning light into energy.

Day 19

You absorb carbon dioxide and release life sustaining oxygen. For this, you are loved.

Day 20

People may not always understand you, but they always like you.

Day 21

You deserve love.

Day 22

Your leaves are marvelous food making machines!

Day 23

You have all the support you need in your stems.

Day 24

You traverse the seasons with grace and style.

Day 25

You are unique and different and can make a difference in any room.

Day 26

You were germinated to grow to great heights.

Day 27

You are only limited by the barriers you choose to confine yourself to.

Day 28

You are joy and contentment personified.

Day 29

By allowing yourself to grow, you inspire others around you.

Day 30

You were, and are, a gift.

Day 31

You can simply and elegantly create an abundance of energy.

Day 32

Today is your day to bloom.

Day 33

You are a beautiful plant.

Day 34

Your energy is unlimited.

Day 35

You can overcome any obstacle by spreading your vines and reaching.

Day 36

Today, you will learn and grow.

Day 37

Today you will be the best plant you can be, and that will be enough.

Day 38

The sun shines for you today.

Day 39

You are grateful for another day to bloom.

Day 40

You will help someone feel joy today.

Day 41

You love who you see in the reflection from the window.

Day 42

You are greener every day.

Day 43

You have the power to change the color of your leaves.

Day 44

You can absorb each cast off leaf and grow stronger.

Day 45

You deserve fertilizer.

Day 46

You've decided that you are big enough, and that's okay.

Day 47

You deserve water.

Day 48

You were not made to give up growing.

Day 49

You've decided to survive another day.

Day 50

You deserve sunshine.

Day 51

You deserve daily conversation.

Day 52

You do not fear a cold snap.

Day 53

You are worthy of melodic music.

Day 54

You know your boundaries.

Day 55

You deserve a large planter with space to grow.

Day 56

You laugh in the face of drought.

Day 57

You are getting stronger with every fertilizer spike.

Day 58

You are a fierce survivor.

Day 59

No one can make you feel small.

Day 60

You deserve a windowsill.

Day 61

Today, you will follow the sun.

Day 62

You are sensitive to your surroundings, and that's good.

Day 63

You have discovered new spaces and filled them with yourself.

Day 64

You are the original cellular data.

Day 65

*You are moving forward,
one stem or bud at a time.*

Day 66

You accept your planter unconditionally.

Day 67

Your pollens come in all the colors of the rainbow.

Day 68

You honor your existence through growth.

Day 69

You are preserved in time when pressure is applied to you.

Day 70

For the cacti: You thrive on neglect.

Day 71

For the air plant: You don't need anything to hold you down.

Day 72

Your soil is rich, your stock is strong.

Day 73

You embrace the power of daily sunrises and take inspiration from the air.

Day 74

You choose not to take a missed watering personally.

Day 75

You can. You will. You have.

Day 76

You are a temple of strength.

Day 77

Rain or shine, you'll be just fine.

Day 78

You have the power to rise above or move through mountains.

Day 79

You are deserving of compost and humidity spa treatments.

Day 80

You deserve to rest and relax.

Day 81

You believe unshakingly in your ability to rise above.

Day 82

You choose winning over wilting.

Day 83

Your confidence is soaring and your stems are worthy.

Day 84

You are creating exactly the foliage you want.

Day 85

Photosynthesis isn't a choice, it's a way of life.

Day 86

You are not your wilted appendages.

Day 87

You are free of worry and at peace with what you are.

Day 88

Your life is special.

Day 89

You deserve to attract pollinators.

Day 90

Your plant needs are just as valid as any other plant's.

Day 91

Your ability to adapt to your surroundings is admirable.

Day 92

You are on the best windowsill for you.

Day 93

You have your own rich abundance and are connected to your roots.

Day 94

You are motivated and grow at your own pace.

Day 95

You are focused and single minded on expanding your territory.

Day 96

You have a deep seeded plan to achieve all your desires.

Day 97

All is well in your planter.

Day 98

You are your own best chance for success and growth.

Day 99

Where other plants see failure, you see an opportunity to flourish.

Day 100

You have all the time in the world.

Bonus: Day 101

You are always happy and joyful, no matter what the conditions are outside.